Brigitte and Jean-Pierre Perrin-Chattard

French
Cooking

Translated by Angela Caldwell

EDITIONS JEAN-PAUL GISSEROT
www.editions-gisserot.com

Introduction

This book contains not only recipes that are familiar to everybody but also a few that we have discovered on our travels and considered to be unusual and tasty.

The recipes are a reflection of traditional French cookery. They use and harmoniously blend the flavours of products and produce from every region of France.

Herbs and spices are used sparingly and delicately to avoid altering or masking the flavour of fish, meat or vegetables.

We have tried to select simple recipes, without any ingredients that are difficult to find, often non-essential or expensive.

The terms used in the explanations are part of everyday vocabulary. We have not used any difficult technical words understood only by professional chefs.

The recipes have all been tried and tested by us. For each dish, we looked into the various methods of preparation and discarded any information that was not essential and positive.

We made, tested and often improved the recipes, taking care to hand on, through our text, the know-how that guarantees success.

This little book will take you on a culinary trip through France, from East to West and North to South.

The inexhaustible variety of good French cooking has encouraged us to continue our research into gourmet fare.

So, until we meet again, "bon appétit" as we say.

Brigitte and Jean Pierre Perrin-Chattard

N.B: Unless otherwise specified, the recipes serve six.

STARTERS

Truffle Omelette

Fairly easy
Serves : 2
Preparation time : 10 mins.
Cooking time : 3 - 5 mins. as preferred

Ingredients :
4 eggs, 1 good-sized truffle (20 g), 1 dsp. goose fat, 5 cl cognac,
5 cl crème fraîche, salt and pepper.

Photo : Claustres

Preparation :
   Brush and wash truffle then slice finely. Marinade for one hour in cognac. Set aside a few good pieces to decorate the omelette.

Break eggs and set aside one egg white. Blend yolks and remaining whites with crème fraîche, whisking well. Season with salt and pepper. Add truffle slices to beaten egg white. Add one dessertspoon of liquid from truffle can or jar.

Melt goose fat in a frying pan and, when it begins to smoke, pour in beaten eggs, after carefully folding in beaten egg white and truffles at the last minute.

Cook over a high heat and serve, folded in three, on a dish decorated with green salad. Decorate omelette with slices of truffle set aside for this purpose.

Quiche lorraine

Easy

Preparation time : 30 mins. including 15 mins. for pastry
Cooking time : 50 mins. including 20 mins. for pastry
Recommended wine : Chablis or Saint-Véran

Ingredients :
300 g wheat flour, 150 g butter, 8 g table salt, 5 eggs, 250 g fromage blanc (60% fat content), 200 g smoked bacon (diced), 1 thick slice ham (150 g, diced), 1 pinch thyme, 1 small onion (puréed), 1 scrape nutmeg, salt and pepper.

Preparation :
   Pastry : put flour in a mixing bowl. Form a well in centre and place softened butter in it (in small pieces), with salt and one beaten egg. Carefully blend ingredients, using your fingertips. When ingredients have been blended, make a ball of dough then break off small pieces of dough and knead in the palm of your hands until smooth (this is called fraiser). Form dough back into a large ball again then leave in a cool place for a few hours, in a lightly floured cloth.

   Quiche : in a mixing bowl, combine beaten eggs, fromage blanc, diced smoked bacon and ham, puréed onion, scrape of nutmeg, pinch of thyme, salt and pepper. Roll out pastry to half a centimetre thick and line a well-greased tin. Prick base with a fork and pre-bake in a medium oven for twenty minutes. When shortcrust pastry is cooked, pour in filling mixture, spreading diced bacon and ham evenly over the quiche.

Return to a medium oven for approximately thirty minutes until the surface is golden brown. Serve piping hot with a side salad.

Warm Goat Cheese Salad

Easy
Serves : 4
Preparation time : 15 mins.
Cooking time : 12 mins.

Ingredients :
300 g mixed salad (escarole chicory, treviso, frisée lettuce), 2 small
white onions (chopped), 2 goat cheeses (crottins de chèvre), 4 slices
bread cut diagonally, 60 g butter, 20 walnut kernels, chives,
4 dsp. walnut oil (or groundnut oil), 2 dsp. wine vinegar,
1 dsp. mustard, salt and pepper.

Preparation :
  Wrap goat cheeses in aluminium foil and place in a hot oven for
twelve minutes (turn them after seven minutes). Remove from oven
and cut in half. Fry slices of bread in butter. In a salad bowl, mix mustard, oil, vinegar, chives, chopped onions, salt and pepper.
  Mix lettuce and walnut kernels, turning gently in the dressing. Add
slices of fried bread and halves of goat cheese.

Mountain Salad

Easy

Serves : 2
Preparation time : 20 mins.
Cooking time (eggs) : 5 mins.

Ingredients :
200 g mixed salad (frisée lettuce,
rocket, treviso, cos lettuce), 2 eggs,
1 glass white wine, 80 g parma-style
ham, 1 slice smoked bacon (diced),
8 slices smoked sausage, 80 g
Tomme de Savoie cheese (diced),
12 walnut kernels, 2 cherry tomatoes
for decoration, 4 small fried croutons, 80 g butter, 4 dsp. walnut oil
(or groundnut oil), 2 dsp. wine
vinegar, 1 dsp. crème fraîche,
1 dsp. mustard, chives, salt and
pepper.

Preparation :
Dressing : put mustard and crème
fraîche in a bowl. Gradually blend
in oil then add vinegar, salt, pepper and chives.

Salad: Place washed, dried lettuce leaves on individual plates. Sprinkle
with vinaigrette and serve remainder separately, in a sauceboat.
Alternate small slices of parma-style ham, diced smoked bacon, slices

of sausage, small cubes of cheese, walnut kernels and small croutons fried in butter. Decorate with cherry tomatoes. Just before serving, add eggs, poached for 5 minutes in a pan of simmering water containing one glass white wine and some salt and pepper.

Cheese "Soufflé"

Fairly easy
Preparation time : 15 mins.
Cooking time : 30 mins.
Recommended wine : Saint-Véran

Ingredients:
70 g butter, 50 g flour,
25 cl milk, 5 egg yolks 6 egg
whites (stiffly beaten),
2 scrapes nutmeg,
100g comté cheese (finely
grated), salt and pepper.

Preparation :

Bring milk to boil. Meanwhile, soften 50 g butter in a saucepan and pour in flour, stirring continuously with a wooden spoon. Place over a gentle heat. When butter/flour mixture begins to froth, pour in boiling milk, whisking all the time. Continue to whisk and bring to boil then turn off the heat as soon as sauce begins to thicken.

Leave mixture to cool slightly then beat in egg yolks and comté cheese. Season with salt and pepper and add nutmeg. Set aside. Beat egg whites to form stiff peaks. Generously butter a soufflé mould, up to the top. Gently fold egg whites into soufflé mixture. Pour into mould, filling it three-quarters full.

Cook for twenty to twenty-five minutes in a moderate oven so that soufflé rises to its maximum. Serve immediately. The comté can be replaced by other cheeses (e.g. Roquefort blue cheese, Swiss cheese or cantal).

You can make other soufflés, for example with seafood or mushrooms, using the same basic recipe.

Gratinéed Onion Soup

Fairly easy

Preparation time : 15 mins.

Cooking time : 40 mins.

Recommended wine : Chablis or White Sancerre

Ingredients :

500 g brown onions (thinly sliced), 1 large potato (cut into eight pieces), 250 g grated Swiss cheese, 1 bouquet garni (thyme, bay leaf), 25 g butter, 4 spoons groundnut oil, salt, pepper, half a

loaf (sliced and toasted), one glass dry white wine (optional).

Preparation :

Cook onions over a gentle heat until golden brown in a cast-iron stockpot in a mixture of butter and oil. Pour in one and a half litres boiling water. Add pieces of potato and season with salt and pepper.

Simmer for twenty minutes with bouquet garni. Remove pieces of potato and mash then blend back into soup. Pour into gratin dish. Lay slices of toasted bread on top. Sprinkle generously with grated Swiss cheese and place in a medium oven for twenty minutes until crispy on top. Do not allow to brown.

Pumpkin Soup

Easy

Preparation time : 10 mins.

Cooking time : 20 mins. (or 6 mins. in a pressure cooker).

Ingredients :

1,5 kg pumpkin (preferably orange-skinned), 1 onion, 2 dsp. crème fraîche, a few peppercorns, 1 small pinch cayenne pepper, 75 cl milk, salt, pepper, paprika, 1 sprig thyme.

Preparation :

Peel pumpkin and cut into large pieces. Season lightly with salt and steam with onion, peppercorns and sprig of thyme for twenty minutes (six minutes in a pressure cooker). Drain, remove and discard sprig of thyme, peppercorns and onion. Strain through a ricer or blitz in a blender, mixing in milk. Put back over a gentle heat.

Check seasoning (paprika, salt,pepper and other spices to taste) and serve hot, blending in crème fraîche at the last minute.

<u>MEAT</u>

Black Pudding with Apple

Easy (if the sausage has already been prepared by your butcher)
Preparation time : 10 mins.
Cooking time : 6 mins.
Recommended drink : Dry cider

Ingredients:
1. Black sausage (home-made):1 litre pig's blood, 1 dribble vinegar to slow coagulation, 300 g fatty bacon with good white fat, 1 large onion, 0,5 apple (puréed),
1 pinch thyme, 1 pig's intestine (well washed and softened), 1 small glass calvados (apple brandy), salt and pepper.

2. Apple puree: 1,5 kg apples (sharp and not too ripe), 10 lumps sugar, 50 g butter, salt and pepper.

Preparation :

1. Mix ingredients, knot one end of pigs intestine and fill with mixture. Press lightly and tie off remaining end. Bring a pan of salted water to the boil, add a small glass of calvados and a bouquet garni (thyme and bay leaves) then boil the sausage for 30 mins. Once cooked, allow to cool for several hours so that it firms up and holds its shape.

Prick with a fork then grill or fry.

2. Peel apples and cut into small pieces. Place in a saucepan, add sugar, salt and pepper then pour in one glass of water. Stir with a wooden spoon and mix in a large knob of butter. Cook for approximately twenty minutes over a gentle heat until the apples have reduced to form a good pale golden puree. Keep warm while you cook the black sausage.

Veal Stew

Fairly easy

Preparation time: 15 mins.

Cooking time : 1 hr.

Recommended wine : Bourgueil

Ingredients :

1 kg veal (breast, arm or top of foreshank), 2 marrow bones, 3 carrots, 2 onions, 2 cloves garlic, 2 dsp. flour, 20 cl crème fraîche, 150 g butter, 3 dsp. oil, 3 egg yolks, 1 bouquet garni (thyme, bay leaf, sage), 50 cl dry white wine, salt, pepper.

Preparation :

Melt 50 g butter and oil in a stockpot. Season pieces of veal with salt and pepper then brown in pan with carrots, onions and cloves of garlic. As soon as meat begins to colour, pour in white wine and two glasses water. Add bouquet garni and simmer for thirty minutes over a gentle heat.

Prepare a blond roux with remainder of butter and flour in a saucepan (cf. short Glossary of Cookery Terms). Moisten with some of the cooking liquor. Add blond roux to pan and simmer for a further ten minutes. Add crème fraîche. Reduce over a gentle heat for fifteen minutes. Just before serving, remove pan from heat and bind sauce with egg yolks. Check seasoning and serve with white rice cooked with mild vanilla flavouring.

Nantes–Style Duck with Peas

Fairly easy

Preparation time : **20 mins.**

Cooking time : **1 hr.**

Recommended wine : **Saint-Véran or Muscadet**

Ingredients:

1 Nantes duck (2 kg), 1 slice smoked bacon (diced), 1 kg fresh peas, 10 small white onions, 2 cloves garlic, 3 carrots (sliced), 1 bouquet garni (thyme, bay leaf, rosemary, sage, parsley), 1 pinch thyme, 2 lettuce leaves, 100 g butter, 5 cl oil, 20 cl dry white wine (Muscadet), salt, pepper.

Preparation :

Draw duck and set aside offal (liver, gizzard). Flame and trim if necessary. Season interior well with salt and pepper and stuff with a small knob butter (20 g), 4 small white onions, one clove garlic, a few pieces of diced bacon and a pinch of thyme. Truss duck. In a large stockpot, brown duck in a mixture of butter (50g) and oil until golden on all sides.

Remove duck from pan and discard fat. Place remaining butter in the pan, turn up heat and brown peas, carrots, small onions, clove of garlic and remaining bacon (diced) for five minutes, stirring conti-nuously. When onions begin to turn golden, pour in Muscadet and one glass of water. Lay duck in the middle of peas, add bouquet garni and lettuce leaves, and season with salt and pepper.

Close stockpot and simmer over a gentle heat for approximately fifty minutes, turning duck twice and checking that there is sufficient cooking liquor left so that peas do not burn.

Serve duck surrounded by its vegetables.

Coq au Vin (Brouilly)

Fairly easy
Preparation time : 30 mins.
Cooking time : 1 hr.
Marinade : 24 hrs.
Recommended wine : Brouilly

Ingredients:
1. Marinade: 1 cockerel (2 kg, cut into 8 to 10 pieces), 1 bouquet garni (thyme, bay leaf, parsley, sage),1 carrot (sliced), 1 clove garlic, 1 shallot, 4 white onions, peppercorns, 5cl Marc de Bourgogne, 5cl wine vinegar, 5cl groundnut oil, 50 cl Brouilly, sea salt.
2. Cooking: 100 g butter, 2 dsp. groundnut oil, 300 g button mushrooms, 6 white onions, 1 slice smoked bacon (diced), 2 dsp. flour, 50 cl Brouilly, peppercorns.

Preparation :

1. Rub pieces of poultry with salt then place in a salad bowl and set aside for one hour. Wipe carefully and place in a bowl with bouquet garni, sliced carrot, clove of garlic, shallot, thinly-sliced white onions, peppercorns, Marc de Bourgogne, wine vinegar and groundnut oil. Pour in enough Brouilly to completely cover pieces of poultry then cover bowl with a clean tea towel and leave in a cool place (not in the

fridge) to marinate for twenty-four hours, turning pieces of poultry twice.

2. Drain and dry poultry with a clean cloth then cook in a mixture of butter and oil for a few minutes over a high heat, until golden. Add whole white onions and diced bacon. Cook for a few minutes more than sprinkle meat with flour.

Strain marinade through a conical sieve then pour into stockpot. Add Brouilly, then the sliced carrot, clove of garlic and bouquet garni taken

from the conical sieve. Add whole button mushrooms (washed and brushed) and a few black peppercorns. Cover and simmer for approximately thirty minutes over a medium heat.

Remove pieces of poultry, lay out on a serving dish and keep warm. Check seasoning in sauce. Remove bouquet garni and clove of garlic. Set aside onions, diced bacon, mushrooms and sliced carrots until ready to serve. Strain sauce through a conical sieve and replace on a low heat for a few moments. Arrange mushrooms, onions and carrots around meat then pour on piping hot sauce which should have thickened slightly. Serve with boiled potatoes.

23

Fresh Périgord Foie Gras

Fairly easy

Preparation time : 30 mins.

Prepare one week before required

Cooking time : 35 mins.

Recommended wine : Sauternes or Loupiac

Ingredients :

1 goose liver (it should be as pale as possible but without any hint of yellowing. A perfect liver should be a very pale pinkish cream in colour). 10 g salt for 500 g of liver, white pepper to taste, 1/2 tasting glass of good cognac or armagnac, 1 good-sized truffle(brush well to remove earth), 200 g thinly-sliced bacon fat.

Preparation :

Remove gall and outer skin from liver, carefully open lobes and remove any nerves and blood vessels. Season with salt (be accurate in measuring out required quantity of salt, based on weight of prepared liver). Season with pepper, pour over cognac or armagnac and knead lightly before placing liver in a terrine. Store in a cool place for twenty-four hours (+4° to +6°).

After twenty-four ours, remove foie gras from terrine and knead slightly, adding a few more drops of cognac or armagnac. Leave in a cool place for one hour while preparing the cooking terrine. Line base and sides with thinly-sliced bacon fat it will protect liver against excessive heat. When liver has regained its firm texture, carefully place in cooking terrine.

Dice peeled truffle into regular pieces then, using the long thin blade of a very sharp knife, split liver open lengthways along the middle. Pull edges of the opening back slightly and carefully slip pieces of truffle halfway down into liver through the split. Close split over by tapping with fingertips until surface is smooth again. Cover with a strip of bacon fat and close terrine. Cook in a bain-marie in oven for thirty-five minutes. The water in the bain-marie must never exceed 80°C.

Photo : J-L Robert

Duck Breasts with Chanterelle Mushrooms

Fairly easy

Preparation time :
15 mins.

Cooking time :
10 mins.

Recommended
wine : Bergerac

Ingredients:
3 duck breasts (each weighing approximately 300 g), 1 shallot (chopped), 1 clove garlic (chopped), 1 sprig parsley (chopped), 2 pinches thyme, 50 g butter, 1 dsp. groundnut oil, 10 cl crème fraîche, salt, pepper.

Preparation :
Season duck breasts with salt and pepper, sprinkle with thyme and fry in a lightly-oiled frying pan until golden on each side. The interior should remain pink. Set aside and keep hot.
Meanwhile, season mushrooms with salt and pepper and fry in another frying pan containing a mixture of butter and oil until mushrooms begin to sweat. Add chopped shallot, garlic and parsley. Sprinkle with thyme. Pour fat off from pan, stir in crème fraîche and serve duck breasts on hot plates accompanied by chanterelle mushrooms.

Pepper Steak

Easy

Serves : 4
Preparation time : 10 mins.
Cooking time : 6 mins.
Recommended wine :
Red Bordeaux (Médoc)

Ingredients :
  6 x 150 g pieces steak,
20 g crushed pepper,
25 g butter, 1 dsp. groundnut oil, 1 dribble cognac,
1 onion, caster sugar,
20 cl crème fraîche, salt.

Preparation :
Sprinkle salt over pieces of meat then roll each one in crushed pepper
on a plate (retain any pepper remaining on plate).
Grease a frying pan with a mixture of butter and oil and fry sliced onion.
As soon as onion begins to turn golden, add pieces of meat and seal over a
high heat for three minutes on each side. Remove from pan and place on
heated plates with sliced onion. Keep plates warm in oven.
Remove frying pan from heat, add a pinch of sugar and deglaze by
flambéing with cognac. Pour in crème fraîche and remaining pepper
from plate.
Turn heat to high and reduce sauce down for a few moments, allo-
wing to boil, until it begins to caramelise slightly.
Pour sauce over meat and serve with French fries.

27

Chicken with Tarragon

Easy

Preparation time : 10 mins.
Cooking time : 1 hr.
Recommended wine : **Saint-Véran or Beaujolais**

Ingredients:
1 chicken (2 kg), 1 small bunch tarragon, 2 white onions, thyme, 20 cl crème fraîche, 80 g butter, 3 dsp. groundnut oil, 5 cl cognac, salt, pepper.

Preparation :
Stuff chicken with a knob of butter, one-quarter of the bunch of tarragon, one onion cut into pieces, a pinch of thyme, salt and pepper.

Brush outside of chicken with oil, season with salt and pepper and sprinkle with thyme. Brown chicken on all sides in a stockpot, in a mixture of butter and oil. Add an onion when chicken is just beginning to turn golden then flambé with cognac. Add two glasses of water and remainder of tarragon.

Cook for approximately forty minutes, turning twice. Remove chicken from stockpot and cut into eight pieces. Reduce remaining cooking liquor by one-half then blend in cream, beating well. Put pieces of chicken back in stockpot and simmer for ten minutes over a gentle heat.

Serve piping hot.

Quercy–Style Tournedos

Easy

Preparation time : 5 mins.
Cooking time : 8 mins.
Recommended wine : **Great red Bordeaux (St Emilion)**

Ingredients:
6 tournedos sliced in the fillet (150 g each), 250 g foie gras with truffle, 30 g goose fat, salt, pepper.

Preparation :
  Heat a skillet and grease well with goose fat. Sear steak over a high heat and cook for four minutes on each side (turning twice). Lay out on heated plates and serve with salad garnish and sauté potatoes. Just before serving, place a slice of foie gras one centimetre thick on each steak.

FISH and SHELLFISH

Grilled Rock Lobster

Fairly easy

Serves : 4

Preparation time : 15 mins.

Cooking time : 15 mins.

Recommended wine : Muscadet sur Lie or Figari blanc

Ingredients :

4 rock lobsters (approx. 400 g each), 8 tsp. crème fraîche, 1 pinch thyme, 1 small shallot (chopped), 1 pinch cayenne pepper, 1 dsp. mustard, 1 dsp. myrtle liqueur (or cognac), 1 pinch fennel seeds, salt and pepper.

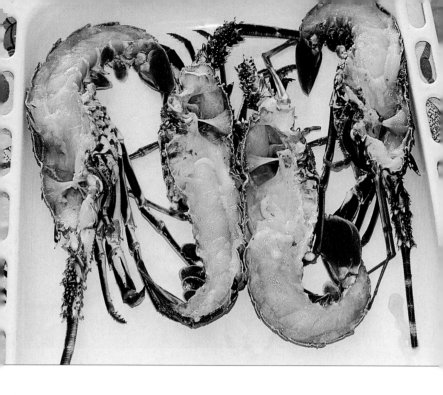

Preparation :

Place rock lobsters on a board and split them open lengthways. Begin by stabbing a strong knife blade into animals chest to kill it instantly.

Remove gravel sac and set aside coral and roe in a large bowl. Lightly season half rock lobsters with salt and pepper. Mix crème fraîche, mustard and chopped shallot with coral and roe in the bowl. Add 1 tsp. myrtle liqueur, 1 pinch thyme, fennel seeds and pinch of cayenne pepper. Whisk well and spread mixture over the half rock lobsters then lay them out in an ovenproof dish.

Bake in a hot oven for ten minutes, then grill for approximately five minutes until rock lobsters are golden.

Scallop Kebabs

Easy

Preparation time : 10 mins.

Cooking time : 10 mins.

Recommended wine : Entre-deux-Mers

Ingredients :
24 scallops,
4 tomatoes (not
too ripe),
2 green peppers,
1 red pepper,
3 large onions,
1 slice smoked
bacon (cut into
strips 0,5 centi-

metre thick), thyme, olive oil, 0,5 lemon, salt and pepper.

Preparation :

Clean scallops well, retaining only white muscle and coral. Chop onions, tomatoes and peppers into large pieces. If possible, use flat skewers they are easier to turn.

Push a piece of onion onto skewer, then a strip of bacon, a scallop and its coral, a piece of tomato, and a piece of pepper (red or green). Repeat, finishing kebab with a large piece of onion.

When skewers are ready, brush with olive oil, moisten with a dribble of lemon juice, season with salt and pepper, sprinkle lightly with thyme and lay out on a serving dish.

Grill kebabs, preferably over hot embers (or under the grill in the oven if you do not have a barbecue) for ten minutes, turning several times to ensure that kebabs cook regularly on all sides. Serve with white rice.

Burbot "à l'armoricaine"

Fairly easy

Preparation time : 20 mins.
Cooking time : 30 mins.
Recommended wine : Muscadet sur Lie or Gros Plant

Ingredients:
1,5 kg skinned burbot, 3 shallots, 2 cloves garlic, 4 tomatoes (peeled, deseeded and pureed), 1 bouquet garni (thyme, bay leaf, parsley), 1 pinch cayenne pepper, 1 pinch paprika, 200 g butter, 5 cl groundnut oil, 5 cl lambig (apple brandy), 50 cl dry white wine (Muscadet), salt, pepper.

Preparation :
Cut burbot into pieces weighing approximately 150 grams. Season with salt and pepper. Fry gently in a pan with oil and 50 g butter.

When fish has turned golden, pour off excess fat and deglaze pan, flambéing with lambig. Add pureed tomatoes, shallots, cloves garlic (chopped) and bouquet garni. Pour on white wine. Correct seasoning (salt, pepper, paprika, cayenne pepper). Cover and simmer over a gentle heat for approximately twenty minutes.

Meanwhile, cut remaining butter into small pieces. When fish has cooked for twenty minutes, remove lid from pan, take out pieces of burbot, lay on a serving dish and keep hot. Reduce sauce in pan by one-third over a gentle heat then bind sauce by whisking in small knobs of butter.

When sauce is thick and creamy, check seasoning again and pour over pieces of burbot. Serve either with white rice cooked with a vanilla pod or with small boiled potatoes.

Sea–Bass in Salt

Fairly easy

Serves : 4
Preparation time: 15 mins.
Cooking time: 35 mins.
Recommended wine: Gros Plant

Ingredients:

1 sea-bass (1,5 kg), 3 kg sea salt (preferably grey sea salt from Guérande), 100 g butter, 1 bunch parsley, 1 tsp. chopped tarragon, 3 cloves garlic, pepper, fine sea salt.

Preparation :

Prepare the fish (remove scales, gut and wash, but retain roe). Wipe fish carefully. Make stuffing with roe, chopped parsley, tarragon and garlic. Season well with salt and pepper. Stuff fish and sew up stomach. Truss fish in a circle, positioning the head against the tail and holding in place by threading kitchen twine through the gills and a hole in the middle of the fleshy part of the tail.

Cover base of a round casserole with a layer of grey sea salt approximately three centimetres thick. Lay fish on its back on layer of salt and completely cover with remaining salt (none of the sea-bass should be visible). Place casserole in a very hot oven for thirty-five minutes.

Remove very carefully (the heat is intense) then turn fish out onto a wooden board. Strike hard to remove block of salt in which fish has cooked. Gently break up block of salt with a meat tenderiser to release sea-bass. It will be perfectly cooked, full of flavour and not at all salty. Remove skin from fish and serve a piece of fillet and a dessertspoon of stuffing on each preheated plate.

Serve with boiled potatoes or rice lightly flavoured with saffron.

Grilled Lobster

Fairly easy

Preparation time : 10 mins.
Cooking time : 10 mins.
Recommended wine : Muscadet sur Lie

Ingredients:
3 lobster (600 g to 800 g), 20 cl crème fraîche,
1 pinch thyme,
1 small white onion, 1 pinch of cayenne pepper,
1 tsp. mustard,
5 cl lambig or calvados (apple brandy), salt and pepper.

Preparation :

Split lobster in half lengthways. Remove gravel sac from each lobster and discard. Remove coral (creamy grey gland in head) and place in a mortar. Using a pestle, crush coral with onion. Gradually add crème fraîche, mustard, thyme, pinch of cayenne pepper and brandy. Split lobster claws. Season interior of the lobster moderately with salt and pepper then cover with a thin layer of prepared cream mixture.

Preheat oven for ten minutes then place lobster in oven (interior uppermost) and grill for approximately ten minutes (set oven to "Grill" position) until seasoning mixture begins to turn golden. Do not allow to burn.

Mussels "à la marinière"

Mussels cooked in their own juice with onions, shallots and cloves garlic.

Easy

Preparation time: 15 mins.
Cooking time: 10 mins.
Recommended wine:
Muscadet or Gros Plant

Ingredients :
3 kg fresh mussels (care-fully scraped and was-hed), 6 cloves garlic, 3 shallots, 2 onions, 3 sprigs parsley, 1 bouquet garni (thyme, bay leaf, tarragon), 50 g semi-salted butter, 75 cl dry white wine (Muscadet or Gros Plant), salt (if necessary) and pepper.

Preparation :

   Place mussels in a large stockpot. Season well with pepper and, if necessary, add a little salt. Sprinkle with garlic, shallots, onions and parsley (all finely chopped). Add bouquet garni and pour in white wine. Cover and cook over a high heat for eight minutes then blend in butter (cut into small pieces).

   Set back over a high heat for five minutes. Remove bouquet garni and serve mussels in their cooking liquor, in hot soup plates.

Sardines Preserved in Lemon Juice

Easy

Preparation time :
10 mins.
Recommended wine :
Gros Plant
(Leave to marinate
for 12 hours before
serving)

Ingredients :
6 good-sized sardines
(or 12 small),
3 slices lemon, juice
of 2 lemons, 1 white
onion, thyme, dill
(chopped), 1 clove,

olive oil, a few slices of gherkin (finely sliced),
a few mustard seeds, salt and pepper.

Preparation :

Remove scales from sardines and gut. Do not wash them. Wipe
them in a cloth (or kitchen paper). Place in a terrine and season with
salt and pepper. Sprinkle with thyme and chopped dill. Add white
onion (finely sliced), a few mustard seeds, sliced gherkin and a clove.
Pour juice of two whole lemons over fish.

Cover with olive oil and leave to marinate for at least twelve hours,
turning once. Decorate with slices of lemon before serving.

John Dory with Sorrel

Easy

Preparation time : 15 mins.
Cooking time : 35 mins. including 15 mins. for court-bouillon
Recommended wine : Chablis

Ingredients:
1 John Dory (1,5 kg), 500 g sorrel, 2 shallots, 2 onions, 6 slices bread,
100 g semi-salted butter, 20 cl crème fraîche, 25 cl water, 25 cl cider,
15 cl dry white wine, 1 bouquet garni (thyme, bay leaf, parsley), salt
and pepper.

Preparation :
   Gut and wash fish. In a pan, prepare a court-bouillon as follows :
   Pour cider, white wine and water into pan. Add a handful of sorrel,
chopped shallots and bouquet garni. Season with salt and pepper. Bring
to boil and simmer for fifteen minutes then strain through a conical
sieve. Lay John Dory in a sauté pan and cover with court-bouillon. Heat
to simmering point and cook for twenty minutes over a gentle heat.
When cooking time is up, take fish out of pan, remove skin and lift off
fillets, keeping them warm in oven on a serving dish.

Creamed sorrel: melt thirty grams butter in a frying pan and fry remaining sorrel after carefully removing the stalks and chopping it finely. When sorrel has reduced to a fine puree, pour on ten centilitres of court-bouillon then twenty centilitres crème fraîche. Season with salt and pepper. Reduce sauce by one-third and pour round the John Dory fillets. Serve with slices of bread fried in butter and rubbed with white onion.

VEGETABLES

Mashed Potatoes

Easy

Serves : 4
Preparation time : 8 mins.
Cooking time : 25 mins. (or 15 mins. in a pressure cooker)
Ingredients :

1 kg potatoes (Bintje or Sirtema), 25 cl milk, 50 g butter, 1 egg, salt and pepper.

Preparation :

Wash potatoes but do not peel. Cook in boiling water seasoned with salt and pepper for twenty to thirty minutes depending on size of potatoes (ten to fifteen minutes in a pressure cooker). Drain, peel and mash with a fork or a potato ricer. Place mashed potatoes in a saucepan, add milk, stirring all the time until the desired consistency is reached. Heat over a gentle heat for a few minutes. Blend in butter, egg, salt and pepper. Mix well and serve piping hot.

Gratin Dauphinois

Fairly easy

Preparation time : 10 mins.
Cooking time : 60 90 mins.
(cooking time depends on the variety of potato)

Ingredients :
1 kg potatoes (preferably Bintje or Sirtema), 500 g fromage blanc (with
60% fat content), 1 large onion (finely sliced), 1 clove garlic, 2 scrapes
nutmeg, thyme, 1 glass dry white wine, 1 slice smoked bacon cut into
small cubes (optional), salt, pepper.

Preparation :

Peel, wash and
dry potatoes then
slice thinly. Rub an
ovenproof dish
with garlic. Butter
dish and cover
base with a layer
of thinly-sliced onions. Follow with a layer of potatoes. Season with
salt and pepper and sprinkle lightly with thyme. Cover with a layer of
fromage blanc. If liked, add a few cubes of bacon. Repeat (i.e. add
another layer of onion, a layer of potatoes, a layer of fromage blanc,
season with salt and pepper, sprinkle with thyme and add diced
bacon if liked).

End with a layer of potatoes and pour on white wine. Add a few
more onions and season again with salt and pepper.

Spread a final layer of fromage blanc on top, season again with salt
and pepper and cook in a medium oven for at least one hour.

Potatoes "à la lyonnaise"

Easy

Preparation time : 15 mins.

Cooking time : 30 mins.

Ingredients :

1 kg potatoes (Bintje or Sirtema, peeled and thickly sliced), 3 onions (thickly sliced), 1 sprig parsley (chopped), 1 small clove garlic (chopped), thyme, 1 bay leaf, 100 g butter, 2 dsp. groundnut oil, 1 dsp. strong mustard, 1 slice smoked bacon (diced), 15 cl crème fraîche, 15 cl dry white wine, salt, pepper.

Preparation :

In an ovenproof casserole with lid, fry potatoes then onions gently for ten minutes in butter and oil mixture. Season with salt and pepper. Add diced bacon and crème fraîche. Heat for a few moments. Dissolve 1 dsp. strong mustard in dry white wine then pour into potato, onion and bacon mixture. Add chopped garlic and parsley, bay leaf and thyme. Close and bake in a medium oven for thirty minutes, gently stirring twice during cooking time. Prick potatoes with a fork to check that they are cooked (cooking time varies from one variety to another).

Peas with Bacon

Easy

Preparation time : 15 mins.
Cooking time : 25 mins. (or 10 mins. in a pressure cooker)

Ingredients:
1,5 kg peas, 1 carrot (sliced), 0,5 bunch spring onions, 1 thick slice smoked bacon, 1 bouquet garni (thyme, bay leaf), 50 g butter, 1 dsp. groundnut oil, 3 large lettuce leaves, 1 sugar lump if peas are not sweet enough (early or winter peas), salt, pepper.

Preparation :

Fry the following in a mixture of butter and groundnut oil, in this order: diced bacon, sliced carrot and white onions. Continue frying until onions begin to sweat then add peas and stir over a high heat until peas turn dark green in colour. Season with salt (handful of sea salt) and pepper to taste then add bouquet garni, lettuce leaves and sugar lump if used. Pour in 40 cl water.

Cover saucepan and simmer over a gentle heat for twenty to twenty-five minutes depending on size of peas. If using a pressure cooker, cook for ten to twelve minutes. Remove lid and stand pan over a gentle heat for a few minutes, if necessary, to allow excess water to evaporate. Serve with roast veal, duck or pigeon.

<u>DESSERTS</u>

Chocolate Mousse

Very easy

Preparation time : 10 mins.
Recommended wine : Barsac
Leave in a cool place for at least 4 hrs. before serving.

Ingredients :
200 g dark chocolate, 4 eggs, 3 dsp.
sugar, 75 g butter, 1 tsp. natural
vanilla extract, a few chopped hazelnuts or almonds (optional).

Preparation :
   Break chocolate into pieces and
place in a saucepan with a dribble of
water. Soften over a gentle heat.
Remove saucepan from heat and add
sugar, egg whites and teaspoon of
vanilla extract, stirring with a wooden spoon until smooth. Mix in softened butter. Beat egg whites until
very stiff then fold carefully into
chocolate mixture.

Photo : J-L Robert

   Pour into small ramekins and decorate with whole blanched almonds
or hazelnuts, if liked. Leave in a cool place for at least four hours before
serving.

Dessert Pancakes

Fairly easy

For 20 pancakes (approximately)

Recommended drink : **Dry cider**

Ingredients:

60 g buckwheat flour, 300 g wheat flour, 100 g castor sugar, 4 eggs, 100 g semi-salted butter, 50 cl milk, 5 cl rum, water.

Preparation :

Put two types of flour in a large mixing bowl. Make a well in centre and fill with beaten eggs and sugar. Begin to work batter with a little water then gradually add milk until batter is smooth. Add melted butter and rum. If batter seems too thick, add a little more water.

Leave batter to stand at room temperature for several hours before use.

Using a pancake pan ("bilig" in Breton) or a heavy-bottomed frying pan, melt a knob of butter and spread it over the surface of the pan using a piece of bacon fat.

Pour in just enough batter to cover the hot surface. Cook over a high heat for two to three minutes. Turn over, top with a knob of butter and cook again for one or two minutes. Serve quickly with jam or sugar.

Chocolate Cake

Very easy

Preparation time : 10 mins.
Cooking time : 25 mins.
Recommended wine : **Loupiac or Jurançon**

Ingredients:
200 g dark chocolate, 3 dsp. flour, 3 dsp. sugar, 125 g butter, 5 eggs, a few almonds, hazelnuts or walnuts (optional).

Preparation :
  Cut chocolate into pieces and place in a heavy-bottomed saucepan with a dribble of water. Melt over a gentle heat, stirring with a wooden spoon until smooth and thick. Melt butter in the cake tin you intend to use then add melted butter, flour and sugar to chocolate and stir over a gentle heat until mixture comes to the boil.

Remove pan from heat. Leave mixture to cool slightly then blend
in five egg yolks. Beat egg whites until very stiff and carefully fold
into mixture. Pour mixture into greased cake tin and cook for
approximately twenty-five minutes in a hot oven (preheated for ten
minutes). Remove cake from tin then decorate with almonds, whole
hazelnuts or walnut kernels.

Pear Belle Hélène

Easy

Preparation time : 20 mins. + 15 mins. for the vanilla ice cream

Ingredients :
1. Vanilla ice cream :
20 cl full cream milk, 15 cl crème fraîche, 4 egg yolks, 65 g caster sugar, 1 dsp. liquid vanilla extract.

2. Pears :
6 pears, 120 g caster sugar, 120 g dark chocolate, sliced almonds, Chantilly cream.

Preparation :
   1. Put ice cream maker bowl or ice cream tray in freezer on the previous day. In a bowl, place egg yolks, sugar and liquid vanilla extract. Beat with an electric mixer until white.

Mix in crème fraîche. Gently heat milk and gradually blend into egg yolk and sugar mixture. Pour this custard into a saucepan and thicken for two minutes over a medium heat. Do not allow to boil. Leave to cool in refrigerator before placing in freezer for at least three hours, in the ice cream maker or an ice cream tray.

2. Peel pears but do not remove core or stalk. Poach in a pan of water with sugar for twenty minutes. Once cooked, pears will be soft. Melt chocolate in a second saucepan, with a dribble of water.

Put two scoops of vanilla ice cream in each ice cream dish. Place cooked pear in centre (you can use a tinned pear instead). Pour melted chocolate over the top. Cover with Chantilly cream and a few sliced almonds. Serve with wafers or almond tuile biscuits.

Hot Apple Tart

Fairly easy

Preparation time : **40 mins.**
Cooking time : **50 mins.** (including pre-baking of shortcrust pastry)
Recommended wine : **Champagne**

Ingredients:
1. For sweet almond shortcrust pastry : 200 g wheat flour, 100 g
ground almonds, 150 g butter, 1 dsp. caster sugar, 1 egg (beaten),
15 to 20 cl water, 8 to 10 g table salt.

2. For tart : 2 kg rustic apples (1 kg to be regularly sliced and 1 kg to
be pureed by cooking with 100 g butter, 150 g sugar and 1 vanilla
pod until soft), 50 g sugar, 10 cl calvados (apple brandy),
25 cl crème fraîche, 1 egg yolk (beaten).

Preparation :
   1. Place flour and ground almonds in a bowl, make a well in centre and add butter (cut into small knobs), sugar, salt, beaten egg then
water. Delicately mix ingredients with fingertips.
   When flour and almonds are blended into other ingredients, roll
dough into a ball then take small pieces of dough in the palm of the
hands and work until smooth (this is called fraiser).
   Form a single ball again with pieces of dough then repeat the operation. Form one large ball of dough and leave in a cool place for a
few hours, wrapped in a cloth dusted lightly with flour.

   2. Roll dough out on a lightly floured pastry board to half a centimetre thick. Carefully grease cake tin with butter and line with pastry.

Prick base regularly with a fork and pre-bake for twenty minutes in a moderate oven. Remove from oven, fill with apple puree then lay slices of apple on top, in concentric circles.

Complete decoration by placing a ball-shaped piece of apple in centre. Pour over five centilitres of warmed apple brandy then flambé. Dampen edges with beaten egg yolk then cook in a hot oven for thirty minutes.

Meanwhile, prepare a caramel with fifty grams sugar. Flavour with five centilitres apple brandy. When tart is cooked and golden brown, pour on caramel and serve with a bowl of whipped cream.

Strawberry Tart

Fairly easy

Preparation time : **30 mins.**
Cooking time: 30 mins . (including pre-baking of shortcrust pastry)

Ingredients:
1. Sweet shortcrust pastry : 300 g flour, 150 g butter, 1 dsp. caster sugar, 1 egg (beaten), 10 g table salt.

2. Tart : 130 g caster sugar (80 g for tart and 50 g for syrup) , 2 eggs, 10 cl milk, 1 pinch salt, 1 pinch natural vanilla (powdered), 750 g strawberries.

Preparation :
1. Place flour in a bowl, make a well in centre and add butter (cut into small knobs), sugar, salt and beaten egg. Delicately mix ingredients with fingertips. When all ingredients are mixed, roll dough into a ball then take small pieces of dough in the palm of the hands and work until smooth (this is called fraiser). Form a single ball again with pieces of dough then repeat the operation. Form one large ball of dough and leave in a cool place for a few hours, wrapped in a cloth dusted lightly with flour.

Roll dough out on a lightly floured pastry board to half a centimetre thick. Carefully grease cake tin with butter and line with pastry.

Prick base regularly with a fork and pre-bake for twenty minutes in a moderate oven.

2. Whip eggs with milk, vanilla, 80 g sugar and 1 pinch salt.
When shortcrust pastry has cooled slightly and is no longer soft,

pour custard into it and put back in oven for ten minutes until custard has set but not coloured. Wash strawberries, carefully drain and remove stalks.

Cut largest strawberries in half and lay out attractively over custard filling. Use remainder of the strawberries to prepare syrup by mashing in a pan with 50 g sugar. Cook over a gentle heat until syrup begins to simmer slightly.

Strain through a conical sieve and brush strawberries on tart with syrup mixture. The same recipe can be used for a raspberry tart.

Table of Contents

INTRODUCTION p.2

STARTERS

Truffle Omelette ....p. 4
Quiche Lorraine ....p. 6
Warm Goat Cheese Salad ....p. 8
Mountain Salad ....p. 10
Cheese Soufflé ....p. 12
Gratinéed Onion Soup ....p. 13
Pumpkin Soup ....p. 14

MEAT

Black pudding with Apple ....p. 16
Veal Stew ....p. 18
Nantes-Style Duck with Peas ....p. 20
Coq au Vin (Brouilly) ....p. 22
Fresh Périgord Foie Gras ....p. 24
Duck Breasts with Chanterelle Mushrooms ....p. 26
Pepper Steak ....p. 27
Chicken with Tarragon ....p 28
Quercy-Style Tournedos ....p. 30

FISH and SHELLFISH

Grilled Rock Lobster ....p. 32
Scallop Kebabs ....p. 34
Burbot "à l'armoricaine" ....p. 36
Sea-Bass in Salt ....p. 38
Grilled Lobster ....p. 40
Mussels "à la marinière" ....p. 42
Sardines Preserved in Lemon Juice ....p. 43
John Dory with Sorrel ....p. 44

VEGETABLES

Mashed Potato ....p. 46
Gratin Dauphinois ....p. 47
Potatoes "à la lyonnaise" ....p. 48
Peas with Bacon ....p. 50

DESSERTS

Chocolate Mousse ....p. 51
Dessert Pancakes ....p. 52
Chocolate Cake ....p. 54
Pear "Belle Hélène" ....p. 56
Hot Apple Tart ....p. 58
Strawberry Tart ....p. 60

© 2003. Editions Jean-Paul Gisserot
Ouvrage imprimé par Pollina - Luçon 85
n° L59820
Printed in France